CONTEMPORARY'S

Put English To Work

LITERACY LEVEL

INTERACTION AND COMPETENCIES FOR JOB SUCCESS

JANET PODNECKY

SERIES ADVISOR
CAROLE ETCHELLS CROSS

CONTEMPORARY BOOKS

a division of NTC/CONTEMPORARY PUBLISHING GROUP
Lincolnwood, Illinois USA

Publisher: Steve VanThournout
Editorial Director: Cindy Krejcsi
Executive Editor: Mary Jane Maples
Editor: Michael O'Neill
Director, World Languages Publishing: Keith Fry
Art Director: Ophelia M. Chambliss
Cover and Interior Design: Michael Kelly
Fine Art Illustrations: Adam Young
Line Art Illustrations: David Will
Production Manager: Margo Goia

Acknowledgments begin on page vi, which is to be considered
an extension of this copyright page.

ISBN: 0-8092-0919-5

Contents

About This Book

Put English to Work is a seven-level interactive workplace-literacy course for students of English as a second or foreign language. The series spans the entire range of levels usually taught in ESL/EFL programs—from the beginning-literacy level to the high-advanced level. A communicative, competency-based program, *Put English to Work* features an integrated syllabus focusing on workplace competencies, general English-language skills, communicative functions, form, and culture. The content of each text has been carefully planned to meet the curricular, instructional, and level requirements of California's state standards for adult ESL programs.

The format of *Put English to Work* is designed for maximum flexibility and ease of use. Teachers in a variety of programs—from vocational ESL and workplace ESL programs to general ESL programs with a school-to-work focus—will find this series ideal for their instructional needs. In addition, teachers who work with multilevel classes will find these texts useful with almost any combination of levels because of the cross-level coverage of a number of the most important workplace topics. *Put English to Work* consists of the following components:

- Seven student books, from Literacy Level to Level 6
- Seven teacher's guides, one for each level
- Seven audiocassettes, one for each level

Each student book contains a Picture Dictionary at the back—an additional resource offering teachers a variety of strategies for vocabulary building. The teacher's guides contain extension activities, sample lesson plans, and suggestions on adaptation of the materials to a number of different teaching styles and programs, from integration of grammar to using the materials in multilevel settings. The teacher's guides also contain the tapescripts for the audiocassettes, which are available separately.

The philosophy behind *Put English to Work*—spelled out in greater detail in the teacher's guides—is interactive and competency-based. The series places a strong emphasis on developing the four language skills—listening, speaking, reading, and writing—in conjunction with critical thinking, problem solving, and computation skills. An important feature is the incorporation of the SCANS competencies, developed by the Secretary's Commission on Achieving Necessary Skills in a project sponsored by the Department of Labor. In addition, the series focuses on a great number of the competencies within the Comprehensive Adult Student Assessment System (CASAS).

Skills are taught within an integrated framework that emphasizes meaningful and purposeful use of language in realistic contexts to develop communicative competence. Target language, structures, and functions are presented in contexts that are relevant to students' lives. Students need to learn strategies and skills to function in real-life situations—in particular, those related to job search and the workplace. Other situations and life-skill areas are covered as well, notably health, family, and community resources.

The cultural focus of *Put English to Work* not only presents aspects of U.S. culture that many students need to come to grips with, but also allows for a free exchange of ideas about values and situations that people from different cultures naturally view differently. In the process, students learn about the culture that informs the U.S. workplace while understanding that their own cultural perspectives are intrinsically valuable.

Put English to Work Literacy Level is geared toward learners at the preliterate and semiliterate levels. Students at this level generally have no knowledge of English, and they may have absolutely no literacy skills. Some students at this level are non-literate in their native languages, other students are from non-literate cultures, and still others are literate in languages that have a non-Roman alphabet. As a result, students who need work at the level of literacy tend to be a diverse group with very diverse needs.

The Literacy Level text was designed to overlap with the Level 1 text to a certain extent, but the beginning of the Literacy Level treats beginning literacy skills such as letter formation, directionality, copying, tracing, and distinguishing between uppercase and lowercase letters. With mixed literacy-level and beginning-level classes, teachers may wish to use the Level 1 text with certain sections of Literacy Level. Suggestions for use of these levels are provided in the teacher's guides for these levels.

The SCANS competencies targeted in Literacy Level are the Basic Skills (listening, speaking, reading, writing, and computation skills).

Acknowledgments

The authors and publisher of *Put English to Work* would like to thank the consultants, reviewers, and fieldtesters who helped to make this series possible, including Gretchen Bitterlin, San Diego Community College, San Diego, CA; Ann De Cruz; Greta Grossman, New York Association for New Americans, New York, NY; Bet Messmer, Educational Options, Santa Clara, CA; Michael Roddy, Salinas Adult School, Salinas, CA; Federico Salas, North Harris Montgomery County Community College, Houston, TX; Terry Shearer, Houston Community College, Houston, TX. Special thanks to Mark Boone.

Introductory Unit A

Circle.

L	(L)EFT	POLICE	WALK
T	TOP	LETTER	DATE
I	ICE	APRIL	IN	CLINIC
H	HOT	RIGHT	HOSPITAL

Write.

↓L   L   L   _____

→T   T   T   _____

→I   I   I   _____

↓H↓ M M   _____

Circle.

E	(E)MPLOYEE	ENTER	EXIT
F	FIRE	OFF	OFFICE
K	KID	BANK	NICKEL
X	X-RAY	EXIT	TAXI

Write.

Circle.

A	(A)GE	NAME	APARTMENT
M	MEN	LIMIT	WOMEN
V	VERY	LIVE	NOVEMBER
N	NO	DON'T	ON NUMBER

Write.

A A A _____

M M M _____

V V V _____

N N N _____

Circle.

C	ⒸLINIC	SCHOOL	CLOSED
O	OUT	OCTOBER	DOCTOR
U	UP	TURN	SUNDAY	U.S.A.
G	GO	AGE	GAS	EGGS

Write.

C C C _____

O O O _____

U U U _____

G G G _____

Circle.

S	(S)TOP	PASSING	STATE
D	DON'T	ADDRESS	DOCTOR
P	PARK	UP	OPEN
B	BUS	JOB	BIRTH
R	READ	LIBRARY	RIGHT

Write.

S S S _____

D D D _____

P P P _____

B B B _____

R R R _____

Circle.

Q	(Q)UIET	EQUAL	QUARTER
J	JUNE	JOB	JUICE
W	WALK	SAW	WEEK
Y	YEAR	DAY	YES
Z	ZIP CODE	SIZE	ZONE

Write.

Q Q Q _____

J J J _____

W W W _____

Y Y Y _____

Z Z Z _____

Write.

UP ↑

DOWN ↓

_____

_____

STOP

EXIT

_____

_____

MEN

WOMEN

_____

_____

WALK

DON'T WALK

_____

_____

Write.

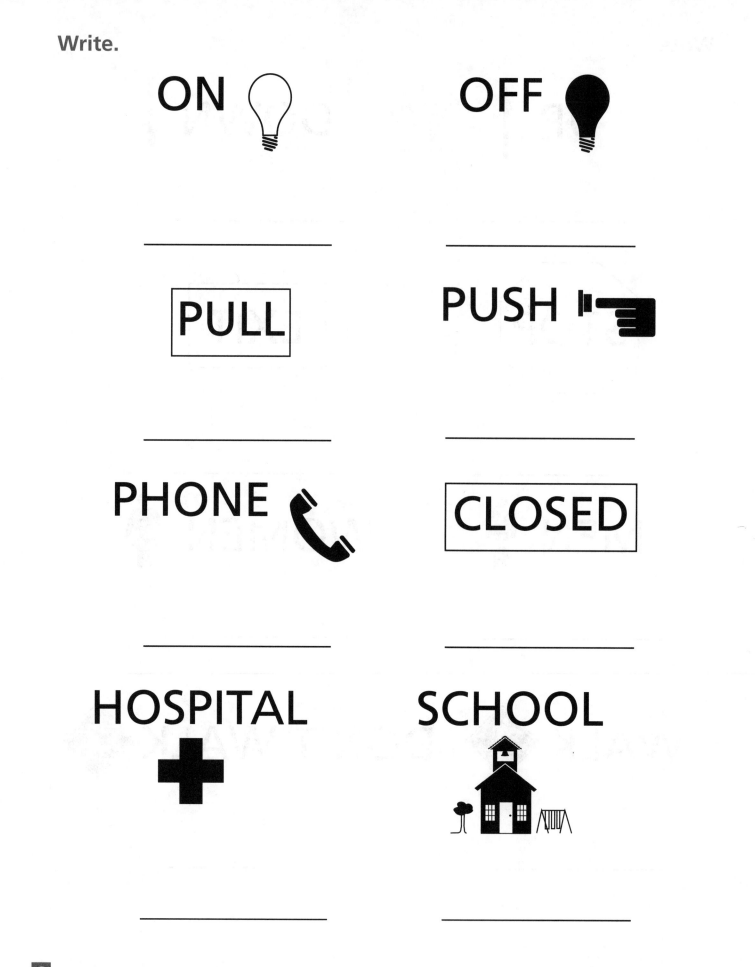

ON

_____

OFF

_____

PULL

_____

PUSH

_____

PHONE

_____

CLOSED

_____

HOSPITAL

_____

SCHOOL

_____

Introductory Unit B

Look. Write. Say.

Aa	Bb	Cc
Dd	Ee	Ff
Gg	Hh	Ii
Jj	Kk	Ll

Mm	Nn	Oo
Pp	Qq	Rr
Ss	Tt	Uu
Vv	Ww	Xx
Yy	Zz	

Circle.

N	a	h	(n)
P	p	g	r
F	t	b	f
L	k	l	i
A	u	a	c
H	h	m	d
R	e	r	k

Match.

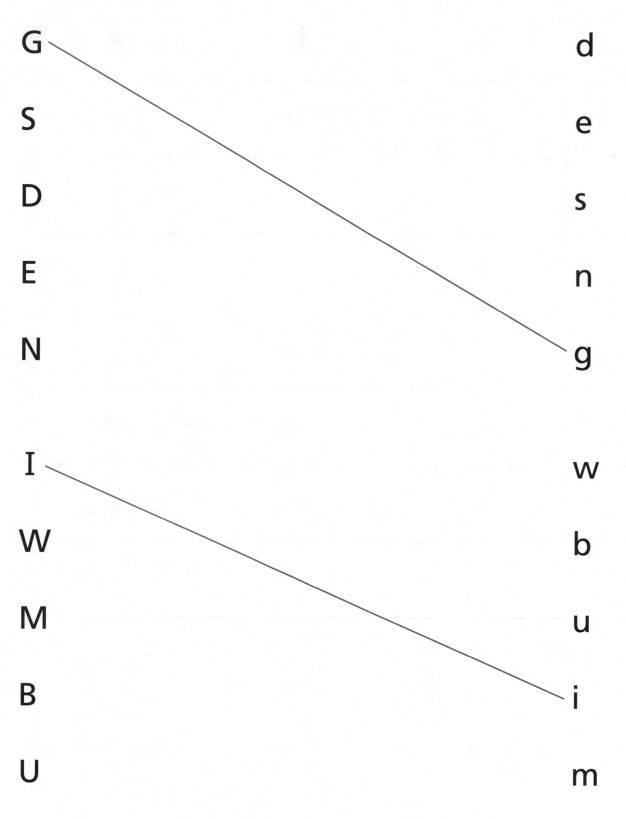

G   d

S   e

D   s

E   n

N   g

I   w

W   b

M   u

B   i

U   m

Look. Write.

0   1   2   3   4   5

0 0 0 _____

1 1 1 _____

2 2 2 _____

3 3 3 _____

4 4 4 _____

5 5 5 _____

Look. Write.

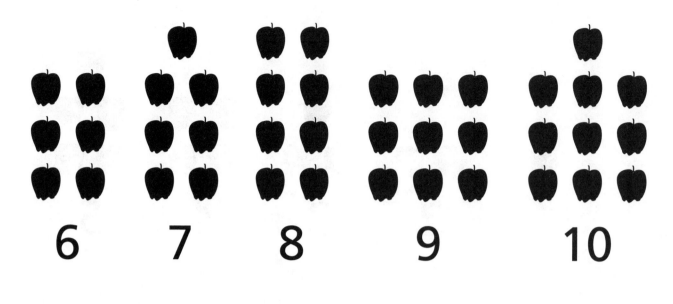

6 7 8 9 10

6 6 6 _____

7 7 7 _____

8 8 8 _____

9 9 9 _____

10 10 10 _____

Circle.

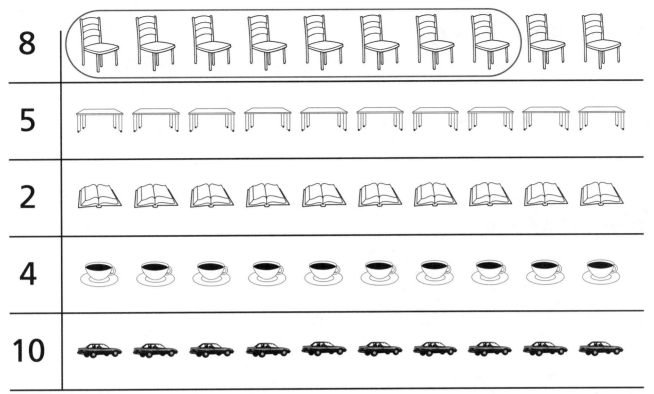

Match.

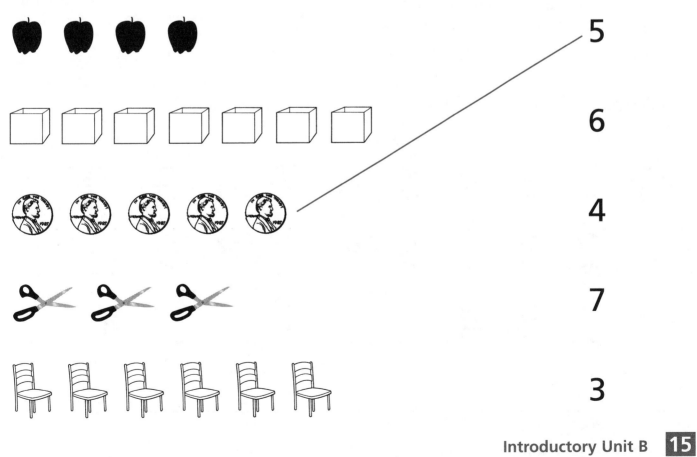

Write.

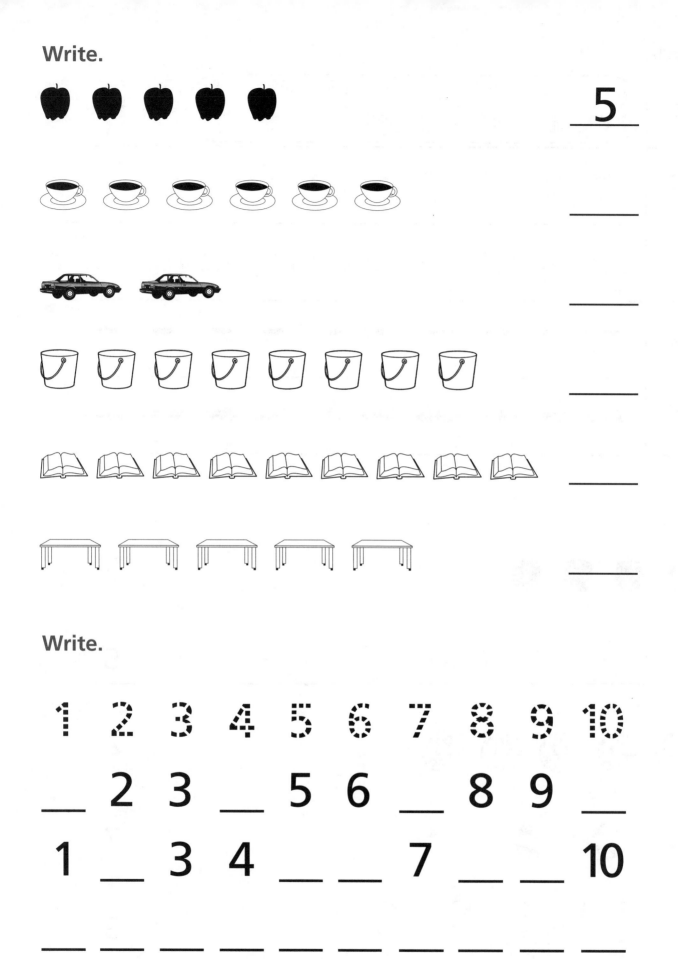

5

_____

_____

_____

_____

_____

Write.

1 2 3 4 5 6 7 8 9 10

___ 2 3 ___ 5 6 ___ 8 9 ___

1 ___ 3 4 ___ ___ 7 ___ ___ 10

___ ___ ___ ___ ___ ___ ___ ___ ___ ___

Unit 1
Hı!

Openers

Look.

1 Listen

Listen. Point.

2 Say

Listen. Repeat.

Marc: Hi. I'm <u>Marc</u>.
        What's your name?
Sonia: My name is <u>Sonia</u>.
Marc: Nice to meet you.
Sonia: And you.

Practice with a partner. Use your name.

3 Read

My first name is Kim. My last name is Lee.

My first name is Bill. My last name is Miller.

Kim Lee

Bill Miller

NAME	Kim	Lee
	First	Last

NAME	Miller	Bill
	Last	First

Circle.

1. NAME	NAM	(NAME)	MANE
2. FIRST	FIRST	FROST	TOAST
3. LAST	LOST	LEFT	LAST
4. Name	Name	Nose	Home
5. First	Fist	First	List
6. Last	East	Last	Late

Match.

1. Name   Kim Lee
2. First Name   Kim Lee
3. Last Name   Kim Lee

4. Name   Bill Miller
5. First Name   Bill Miller
6. Last Name   Bill Miller

4 Listen

Listen. Circle. Write.

1. (B) T   __B__ i l l

2. P   M   _____ a r c

3. L   S   _____ e e

4. D   W   _____ a v i s

5. N   K   _____ i m

6. I   A   _____ n n a

5 Say

My first name is
Bill. B-I-L-L.
My last name is
Miller. M-I-L-L-E-R.

Spell your first name.
Spell your last name.

6 Listen

Listen. Circle.

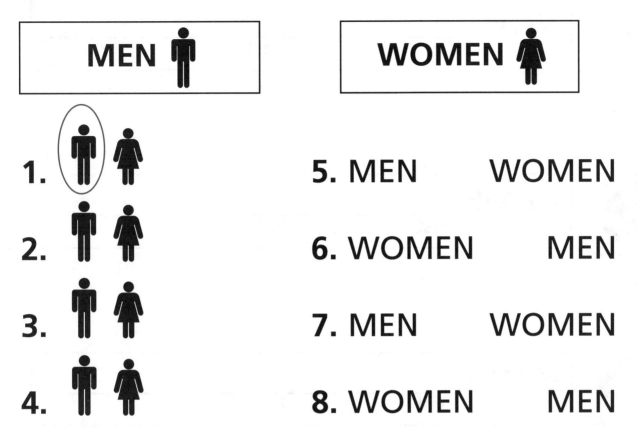

MEN 🧍	WOMEN 🧍‍♀️
1.	5. MEN WOMEN
2.	6. WOMEN MEN
3.	7. MEN WOMEN
4.	8. WOMEN MEN

7 Match

1. MEN 2. WOMEN 3. WOMEN 4. MEN

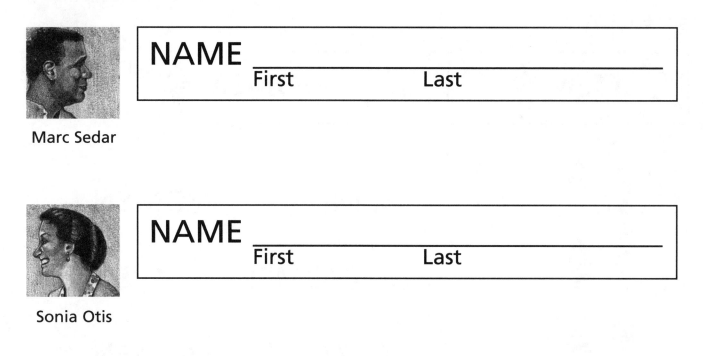

Marc Sedar

NAME _____
      First   Last

Sonia Otis

NAME _____
      First   Last

Kim Lee

NAME _____
      First   Last

What's your name?

NAME _____
      First   Last

NAME _____
      First   Last

Application

1 Listen

Listen and circle.

1. Last (Name)
2. First Last
3. Last First
4. First Name
5. Last First
6. Last First

2 Write

My name is _____.

My first name is _____.

My last name is _____.

Listen and circle.

1. (Ken)   Pen   Ten
2. Take   Lake   Make
3. Peter   Sedar   Pedro
4. Sale   Pole   Nole
5. Han   Can   Dan
6. Eden   Adams   Odell

4 Copy

Sonia Otis   Marc Sedar   Anna Davis   Kim Lee   Bill Miller

WOMEN   MEN

Kim Lee   Bill Miller

_____   _____

_____   _____

Write your name. _____

Unit 2
NUMBERS

Openers

Look.

1 Listen

Listen. Point.

2 Say

Listen. Repeat.

What's your phone number?

731–4289

Practice with a partner. Use your phone number.

3 Read

My name is Kim Lee.
My phone number is
234-5521.

My name is Bill Miller.
My phone number is
521-7890

NAME	Kim	Lee	NAME	Bill	Miller
PHONE NUMBER	234-5521		**PHONE NUMBER**	521-7890	

Circle.

1. 123	312	(123)	132
2. 534	533	453	534
3. 748	748	749	148
4. 963	693	963	968
5. 502	802	582	502
6. 841	841	847	341

Match.

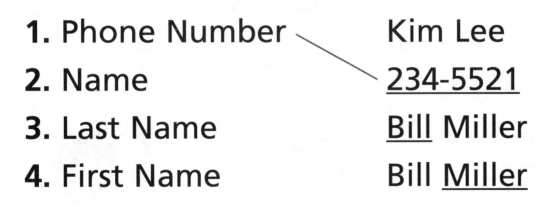

1. Phone Number   Kim Lee

2. Name   <u>234-5521</u>

3. Last Name   <u>Bill</u> Miller

4. First Name   Bill <u>Miller</u>

4 Listen

Listen. Circle.

1. (742-8901)	724-8801
2. 547-9695	527-6685
3. 321-7474	321-4474
4. 695-4312	965-4421
5. 827-3355	927-3255
6. 278-9110	378-9110

Listen. Write.

1. 3__2-__5__9   4. 7__ __-__ __55

2. __31-__46__   5. __ __ __-4357

3. 8__ __-032__   6. 452-__ __ __ __

5 Say

Anna: What's your phone number?
Bill: 742-8901.
Anna: 742-8901?
Bill: Yes. That's right.

What's your phone number?

6 Listen

Look. Listen.

11 12 13 14 15 16 17 18 19 20

Listen. Circle.

1.	12	(15)	18
2.	14	19	13
3.	16	11	20
4.	17	13	19
5.	18	12	16

7 Match

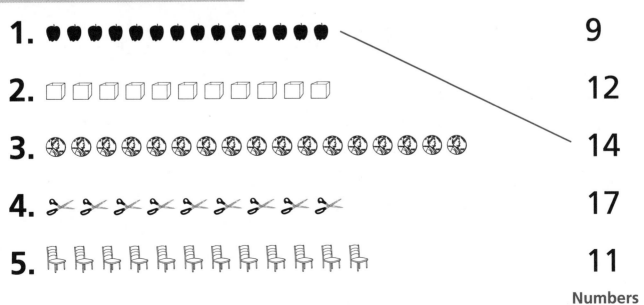

1. ●●●●●●●●●●●●●●   9

2. ▱▱▱▱▱▱▱▱▱▱   12

3. ⊛⊛⊛⊛⊛⊛⊛⊛⊛⊛⊛⊛⊛⊛   14

4. ✂✂✂✂✂✂✂✂   17

5. 🪑🪑🪑🪑🪑🪑🪑🪑🪑🪑🪑   11

1	2	3	4	5	6	7	8	9	10
11	12	13	14	15	16	17	18	19	20

1	__	3	4	__	6	7	__	9	10
__	12	13	__	15	__	17	18	__	__

1	__	__	__	__	__	__	__	__	10
11	__	__	__	__	__	__	__	__	20

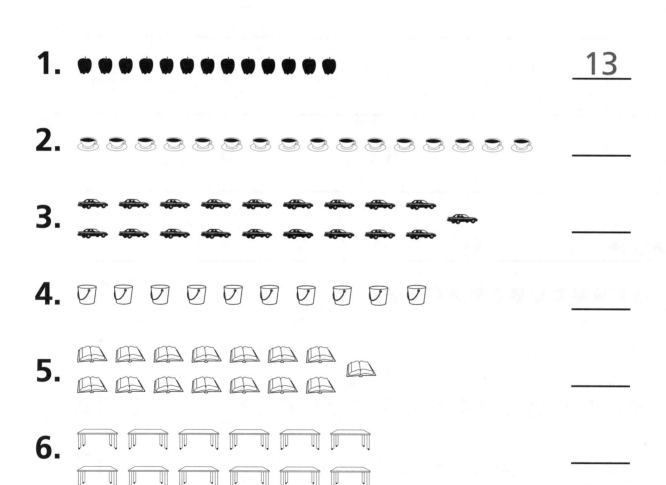

1. ⬛⬛⬛⬛⬛⬛⬛⬛⬛⬛⬛⬛⬛   _13_

2.   ___

3.   ___

4.   ___

5.   ___

6.   ___

1 Listen

Listen and match.

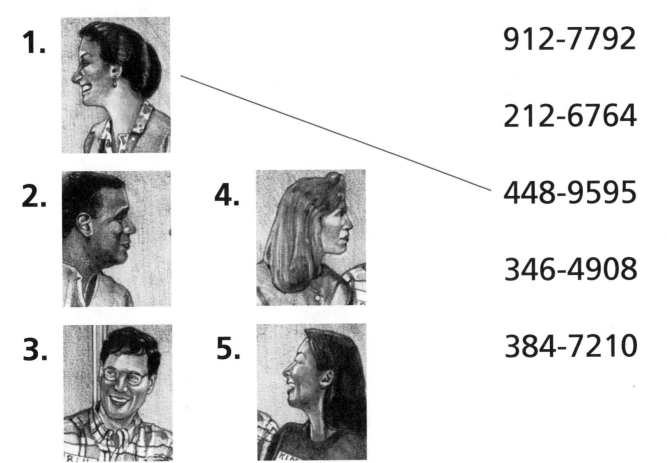

1.   912-7792

2.   4.   212-6764

                        448-9595

                        346-4908

3.   5.   384-7210

2 Write

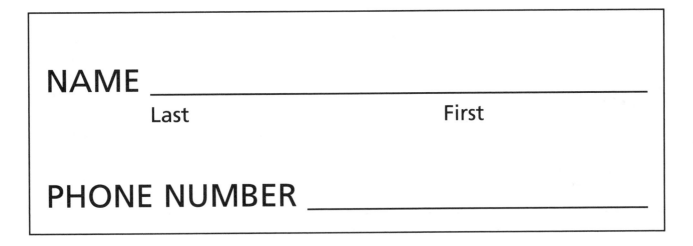

NAME _____

   Last   First

PHONE NUMBER _____

Listen. Circle.

1.	18	(13)	12
2.	14	11	19
3.	12	15	17
4.	19	16	13
5.	15	14	12
6.	16	17	11

4 Copy

IMPORTANT PHONE NUMBERS	
NAME	**PHONE NUMBER**
FIRE	
AMBULANCE	
SCHOOL	

Unit 3
HOME

Openers

Look.

1 Listen

Listen. Point.

2 Say

Listen. Repeat.

What's your address?

114 Pine Street.

Practice with a partner. Use your address.

3 Read

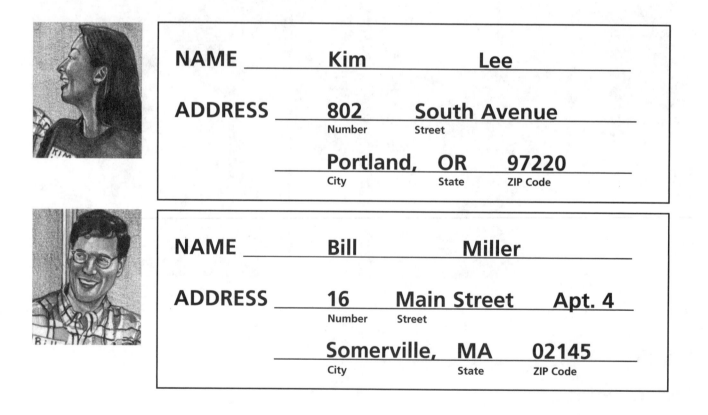

NAME	Kim		Lee	
ADDRESS	802	South Avenue		
	Number	Street		
	Portland,	OR	97220	
	City	State	ZIP Code	

NAME	Bill		Miller	
ADDRESS	16	Main Street	Apt. 4	
	Number	Street		
	Somerville,	MA	02145	
	City	State	ZIP Code	

Circle.

1. ADDRESS	DRESS	(ADDRESS)	APRIL
2. STREET	STATE	TREAT	STREET
3. CITY	CITY	SIGN	CANDY
4. STATE	STATE	TASTE	STEAK
5. ZIP CODE	ZONE	ZIP CODE	ZERO
6. NUMBER	NUMBER	MEMBER	NAME

Draw a line.

Address

City

Name

Sonia Otis

310 Green Street

San Jose, CA 95124

Street

ZIP Code

State

4 Listen

Listen. Circle.

1. (Address)   Street   City
2. ZIP Code   State   Number
3. Street   Name   Phone
4. City   ZIP Code   Address
5. Phone   Street   City
6. Name   Number   ZIP Code

5 Say

A: What's your address?
B: 16 Main Street.
A: City and state?
B: San Jose, California.
A: What's your ZIP code?
B: 95124.

What's your address? Ask a friend.

6 Listen

Look. Listen.

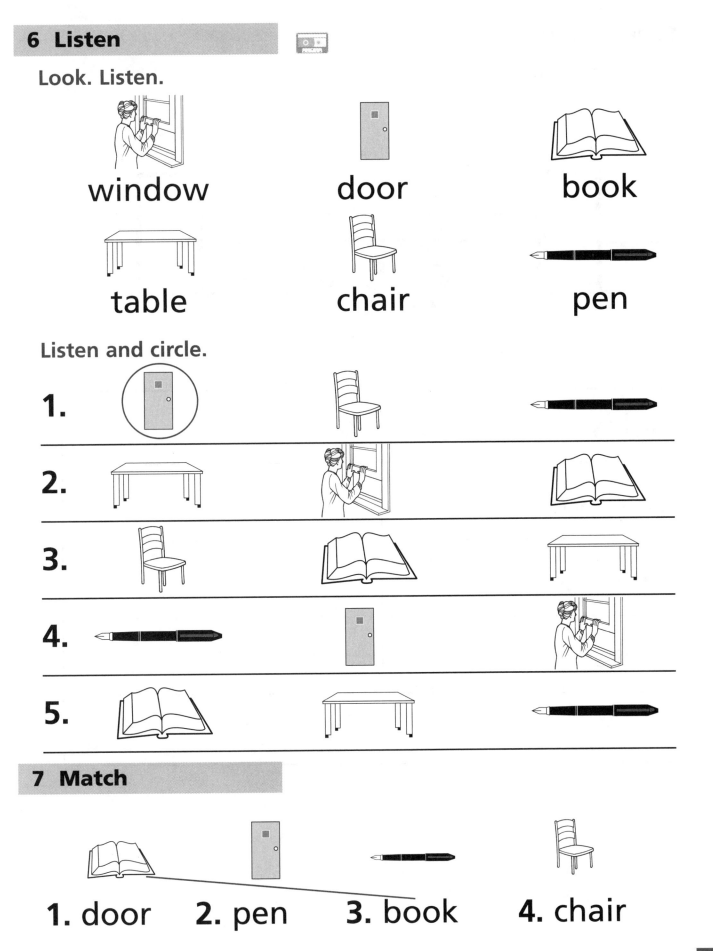

window   door   book

table   chair   pen

Listen and circle.

1.

2.

3.

4.

5.

7 Match

1. door   2. pen   3. book   4. chair

Count. Write the number.

tables	4
windows	
doors	
books	

1 Listen and Match

Listen. Circle and match.

1. (NAME)D	NUMBER	A. 520 Park Street
2. BOX	PHONE	B. Denver
3. APPLE	ADDRESS	C. 06321
4. CITY	SLOW	D. Sonia Otis
5. ZOO	ZIP CODE	E. 384-7210

2 Write

NAME _____

        First   Last

ADDRESS _____

        Number   Street

_____

        City   State   ZIP Code

PHONE NUMBER _____

1. (818 South Street)   713-6214
2. Somerville   04756
3. Kim Lee   MA
4. 713-6214   Somerville
5. 04756   818 South Street
6. MA   Kim Lee

4 Ask and Write

Ask some friends. Write.

ADDRESSES	
NAME	**ADDRESS**
1.	
2.	
3.	

Unit 4
LEFT OR RIGHT?

Look.

1 Listen

Listen. Point.

2 Say

Listen. Repeat.

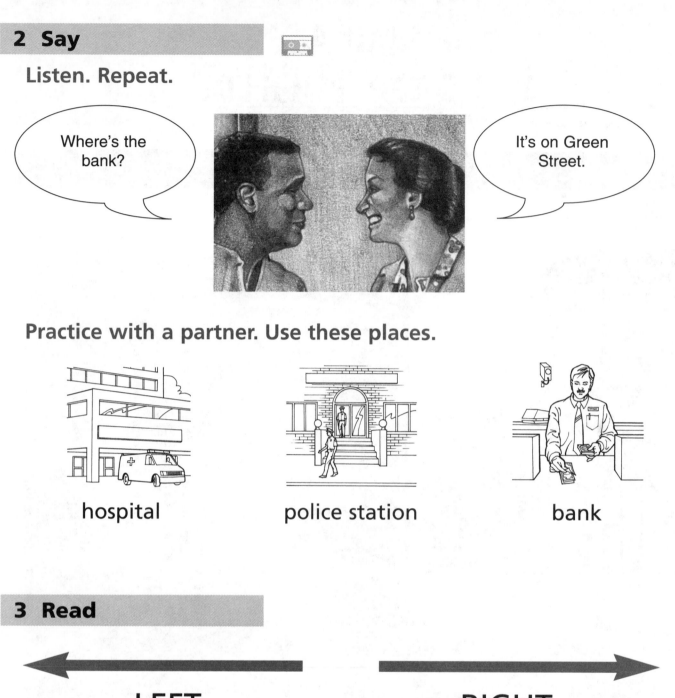

Where's the bank?

It's on Green Street.

Practice with a partner. Use these places.

hospital   police station   bank

3 Read

← **LEFT**   **RIGHT** →

The store is on Green Street.
It's **on the left.**

The post office is on Green Street.
It's **on the right.**

Circle.

1. BANK	FIRST CITY (BANK) & TRUST
2. STORE	D & R FOOD STORE
3. POST OFFICE	U.S. POST OFFICE HARTLAND 05052
4. LIBRARY	HARTLAND PUBLIC LIBRARY
5. HOSPITAL	SPRINGFIELD HOSPITAL
6. SCHOOL	RIVERSIDE HIGH SCHOOL

Match.

1. LIBRARY

2. BANK

3. STORE

4. POST OFFICE

5. HOSPITAL

4 Listen

Listen. Write.

1. BANK

2. STORE

3. HOSPITAL

4. LIBRARY

bank

5 Say

Where's the bank?

It's on the right.

Practice with the other places.

6 Look and Listen

Look. Listen.

1	2	3	4	5	6	7	8	9	10
11	12	13	14	15	16	17	18	19	20
21	22	23	24	25	26	27	28	29	30

Listen. Circle.

1. 25   (27)   20

2. 29   19   21

3. 15   22   24

4. 28   18   23

5. 16   26   29

7 Match

1. □□□□□□□□□ □□□□□□□   20
2. □□□□□□□□ □□□□□□□□□□ □□□□□□   26
3. □□□□□□□□□ □□□□□□□□□□ □   18
4. □□□□□□□□□ □□□□□□□□□   21

8 Write

A.

1	2	3				
	9	10				
					20	21
			25			
	30					

B.

	EXIT	
Room 21		Room 22
Room 23		Room _24_
Room ___		Room ___
Room ___		Room ___
Room ___		Room 30

Application

1 Listen

Listen and circle.

1.

2.

3.

4.

2 Write

office	left	right
Green	bank	Street

The post _____ is on Green Street. It's on the
_____ . The store is on _____ Street. It's on the
_____ . The _____ is on Green _____ .
It's on the left.

Left or Right?   47

3 Listen and Circle

1. (28 Main Street)   25 Main Street
2. 321 Green Street   324 Green Street
3. 729 River Road   722 River Road
4. 520 Adams Avenue   512 Adams Avenue
5. 623 Hope Drive   629 Hope Drive

4 Write

Place	Address	Phone Number
School		
Post Office		
Hospital		
Library		

Unit 5
IT'S TIME

Openers

Look.

1 Listen

A. Listen and point.

B. Listen and repeat.

2 Say

Listen. Repeat.

A: Excuse me,
      what time is it?
B: It's 10:00.
A: Thanks.
B: You're welcome.

Practice with a partner. Use these times.

3 Read

Shop & Save

STORE HOURS

OPEN   CLOSED

7:00–6:00

First City Bank

OPEN 7:00–6:00 Mon.–Fri.

CLOSED Sat./Sun.

Circle.

1.	<clock 7:00>	1:00	3:00	(7:00)
2.	<clock 2:00>	10:00	3:00	2:00
3.	<clock 12:00>	12:00	6:00	1:00
4.	<clock 8:00>	11:00	5:00	8:00

Match.

1.   **2.**   **3.**   **4.**   **5.**

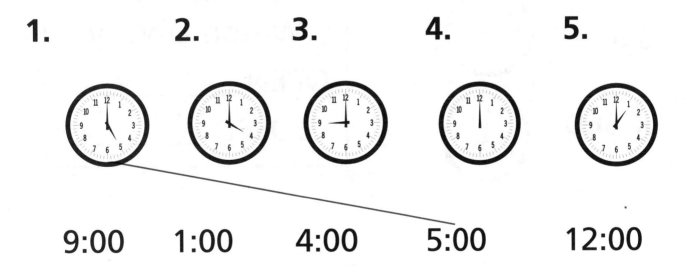

9:00   1:00   4:00   5:00   12:00

OPEN

CLOSED

BANK

OPEN _____

CLOSED _____

OPEN

CLOSED

STORE

OPEN _____

CLOSED _____

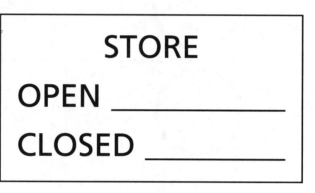

OPEN

CLOSED

Wilson Library

OPEN _____

CLOSED _____

5 Listen and Speak

A: What time does the <u>bank</u> open?
B: <u>9:00</u>.
A: Thank you.
B: You're welcome.

Bank: 9:00–4:00

Practice with a friend.

Post Office: 7:00–5:00

Store: 8:00–8:00

6 Read and Write

U.S. POST OFFICE Hartland OPEN 8:00–5:00	Everett Public Library OPEN 10:00–7:00

1. The post office opens at _____.
2. The library opens at _____.
3. The post office closes at _____.
4. The library closes at _____.

Numbers

Look.

31 32 33   34   35   36   37   38   39   40
41 42 43   50
51   60

1 Listen and Circle

1. (34) 37 42   5. 28 38 18
2. 51 60 46   6. 40 34 47
3. 48 39 52   7. 53 35 39
4. 35 25 45   8. 15 50 55

2 Listen and Write

1. _____   4. _____
2. _____   5. _____
3. _____   6. _____

3 Write

1. 31 ___ 33 34 ___
2. 46 47 ___ 49 ___
3. 54 ___ 56 ___ 58

1 Paperwork

Listen. Write the times.

1.

State Savings Bank

OPEN _____

CLOSED _____

2.

Elm Street Library

OPEN _____

CLOSED _____

3.

U.S. Post Office

OPEN _____

CLOSED _____

4.

Save More Store

OPEN _____

CLOSED _____

2 Write

Write the times.

_____   _____

_____

_____

_____

_____

3 Culture Work

Look.

7:00 A.M.

8:00 P.M.

Unit 6
MY FAMILY

Openers

Look.

1 Listen

A.   Listen and point.

B.   Listen and repeat.

2 Say

Listen. Repeat.

Daughter   Son
Mary   Tom

A: This is my family.
B: Who's that?
A: That's my <u>daughter</u>.
B: Her name is <u>Mary</u>.

Practice with a partner. Talk about your family.

3 Read

Family Information Form

Name   Kim Lee

Family Members

	Name	Age	Relationship
Spouse	Hung-ju Lee	42	husband / wife
Children	Mary Lee	8	daughter
	Tom Lee	7	son

Circle.

1. CHILDREN	CHICKEN	(CHILDREN)	CHILLY
2. HUSBAND	HUNGRY	HUNDRED	HUSBAND
3. WIFE	WIFE	WOMEN	WISE
4. SON	SAME	SON	SIGN
5. DAUGHTER	DAWN	DAUGHTER	BOUGHT

Match.

1. family

2. husband

3. son

4. daughter

5. wife

6. children

My Family

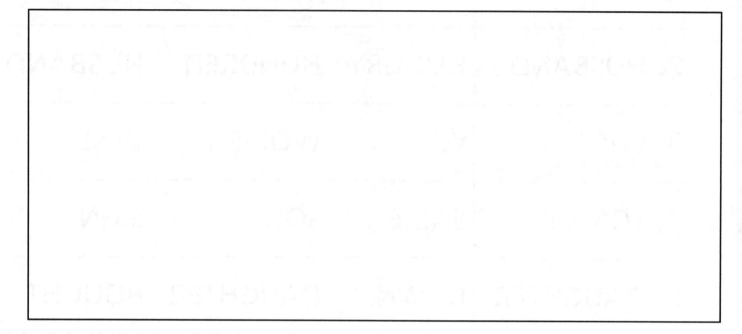

Family Information Form

Name _____

Family Members

Name	Age	Relationship
_____	_____	_____
_____	_____	_____
_____	_____	_____
_____	_____	_____

5 Listen and Speak

A: Is this your <u>brother</u>?
B: Yes, it is.
A: How old is <u>he</u>?
B: <u>He's 22</u>.

Practice with a friend.

father—53, mother—49, brother—22

6 Read and Write

Family Information Form

Name ___Marc___ ___Sedar___   Age ___26___

Family Members

Name	Age	Relationship
Raymond Sedar	52	father
Marie Sedar	50	mother
Tomas Sedar	17	brother
Nancy Sedar	15	sister

---

1. Who is Marc's father? _____.

2. Who is his mother? _____.

3. How old is Nancy? _____.

4. How old is his brother? _____.

Numbers

Look.

10 20 30 40 50 60 70 80 90 100

1 Listen and Circle

1. 60 (70) 50   5. 83 88 82
2. 75 35 45   6. 72 76 79
3. 58 78 28   7. 67 65 63
4. 31 41 81   8. 91 94 97

2 Listen and Write

1. ___77___   4. _____
2. _____   5. _____
3. _____   6. _____

3 Write

81 ___ ___ 84 ___ ___ ___

75 76 ___ ___ 79 ___ 81

10 20 ___ 40 ___ 60 ___ ___ ___ 100

1 Paperwork

Listen. Circle the correct information.

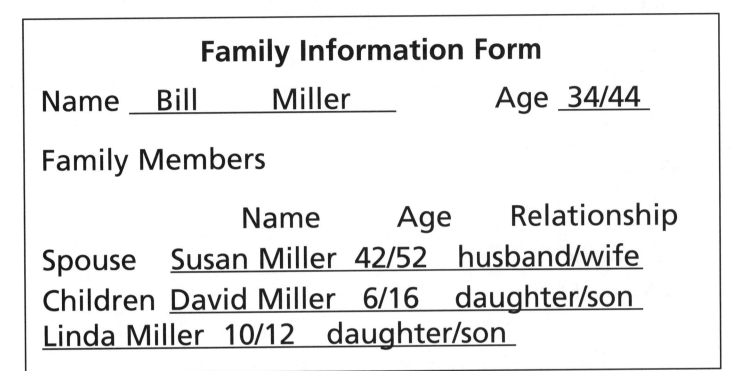

Family Information Form

Name ___Bill___ ___Miller___   Age ___34/44___

Family Members

	Name	Age	Relationship
Spouse	Susan Miller	42/52	husband/wife
Children	David Miller	6/16	daughter/son
	Linda Miller	10/12	daughter/son

2 Pair Work

Ask a friend.

Example: A: Who is that?
           B: John.
           A: How old is he?
           B: He's 35.

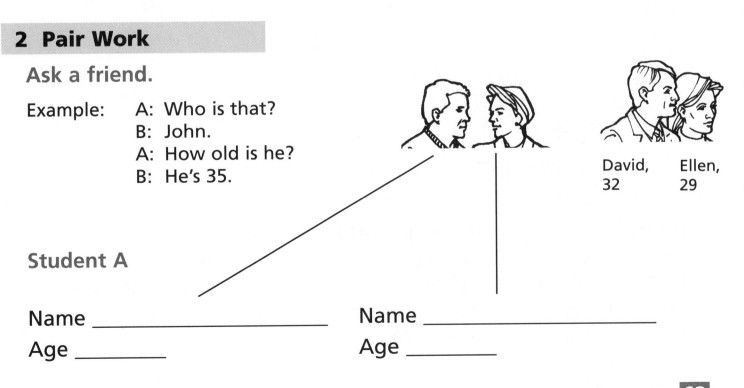

David, 32   Ellen, 29

Student A

Name _____   Name _____

Age _____   Age _____

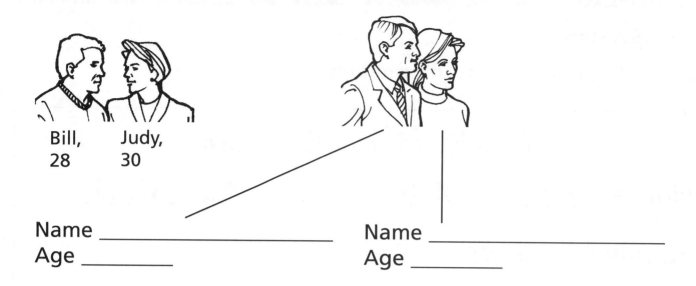

Bill,
28

Judy,
30

Name _____

Age _____

Name _____

Age _____

3 Culture Work

The Nelson Family

NAME	RELATIONSHIP	
Paul Nelson	husband	Mr. Nelson
Denise Nelson	wife	Mrs. Nelson

The Timmons Family

NAME	RELATIONSHIP	
Lou Timmons	husband	Mr. Timmons
Cathy Timmons	wife	Mrs. (or Ms.) Timmons
Stan Timmons	son	Mr. Timmons
Ellen Timmons	daughter	Ms. Timmons

Openers

Look.

1 Listen

A. Listen and point.

B. Listen and repeat.

2 Say

Listen. Repeat.

A: I need a job.
B: What do you do?
A: I'm a <u>cook</u>.
B: Look. Here's an ad
for a <u>cook</u>.

driver

painter

dishwasher

Practice with a partner. Talk about these jobs.

3 Read

HELP WANTED

Painter Mornings 8:00 A.M.–12:00 P.M. Call 655-9275	**Dishwasher** needed Evenings 5:00 P.M.–10:00 P.M. Call 422-5533	**Driver** wanted Afternoons 2:00 P.M.–6:00 P.M. Call 479-8110

Circle the jobs.
Underline the times.
Circle the phone numbers.

Circle.

1. PAINTER	Wanted: Full-time (painter) for house painting.
2. CASHIER	Opening for cashier. No experience needed.
3. COOK	Experienced line cook for busy restaurant.
4. DRIVER	Delivery driver. Must have good driving record.
5. DISHWASHER	Immediate opening for dishwasher. Flexible hours.

Match.

1. painter

2. driver

3. cashier

4. dishwasher

4 Write

A.   Write the jobs.

| dishwasher | cashier | painter |

He's a _____. She's a _____. She's

a _____.

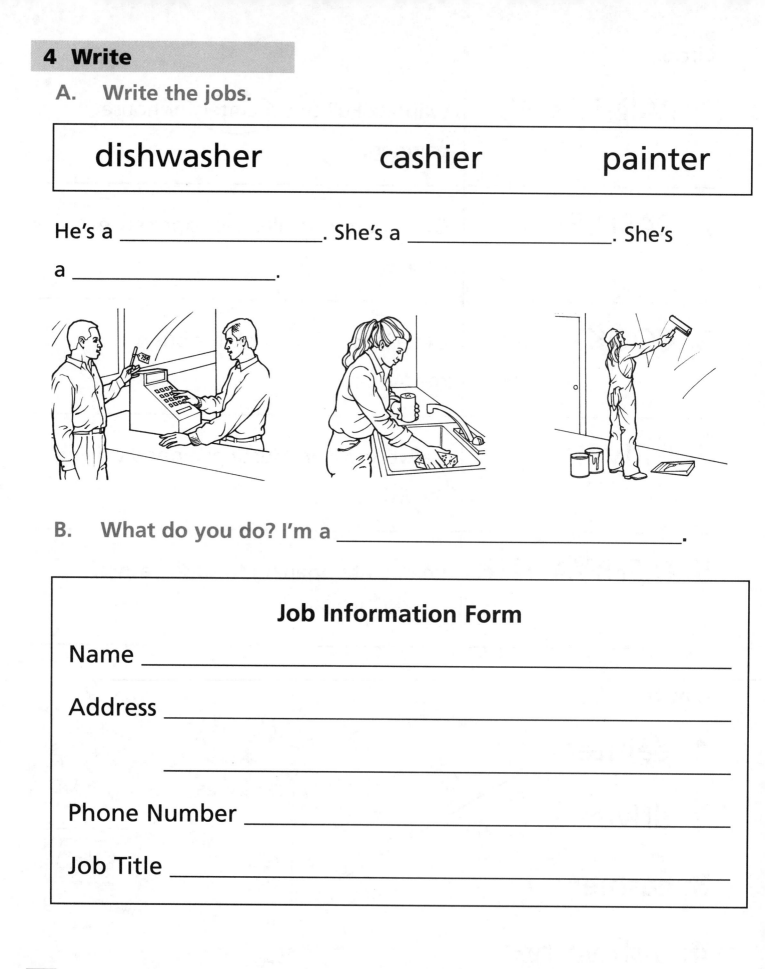

B.   What do you do? I'm a _____.

Job Information Form

Name _____

Address _____

_____

Phone Number _____

Job Title _____

A: What do you do?
B: I am a <u>driver</u>.
What do you do?
A: I'm a <u>painter</u>.

Practice with a friend.

6 Read and Write

Job Application

Name <u>Marc   Sedar</u>   Age <u>26</u>

Address <u>155 West Street</u> Phone <u>437-5561</u>

<u>Somerville, MA 02115</u>

Work Experience

Job Title	Dates	Employer
Cashier	1995–now	Mill Cafe
Cook	1992–1995	Amelia's Restaurant

1. What does Marc do now? He's a _____.
2. Where does he work now? At _____.

Numbers

1 Listen and Circle

1. 1982 (1980) 1922   5. 1919 1991 1908
2. 1993 1939 1930   6. 1981 1971 1961
3. 1975 1965 1995   7. 1963 1986 1946
4. 1998 1988 1990   8. 1985 1955 1975

2 Listen and Write

1. _1973_   4. _____
2. _____   5. _____
3. _____   6. _____

3 Write

| 1993–1997 | 472-6632 | 317 |

Job Application

Name <u>Sonia Otis</u>   Phone _____

Address <u>Garden Avenue</u>

        <u>Boston, MA 02115</u>

Work Experience

Job Title	Dates	Employer
Painter	_____	Steven's Paint Co.

1 Paperwork

Listen. Circle the correct information.

Job Application

Name <u>Marc Sedar</u> **Phone** <u>437-5561 or 437-6615</u>

Address <u>155 West Street</u>

<u>Somerville, MA 02115</u>

Work Experience

Job Title	Dates	Employer
Painter or Dishwasher	1995–Now	Mill Cafe
Cook or Cashier	1992–1995 or 1990–1996	Amelia's Restaurant

---

2 Pair Work

Ask a friend.

Example: A: What's your name?
           B: <u>John Smith</u>.
           A: What do you do?
           B: I'm a <u>driver</u>.

painter	cook	cashier	driver

Jobs in my country	Jobs in the U.S.
cook	cook

Add other jobs you know.

Signs at work. Check the signs you see.

_____ NO SMOKING

_____ FLAMMABLE

_____ POISON

_____ HIGH VOLTAGE

_____ FIRE EXTINGUISHER

Unit 8
MONEY

Openers

Look.

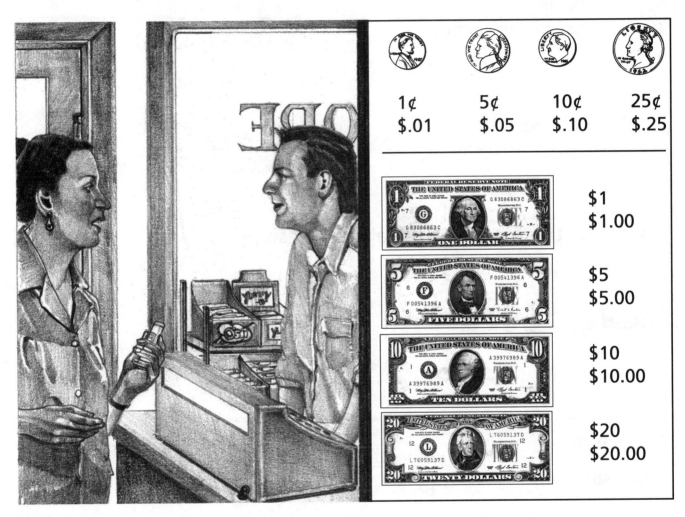

1¢	5¢	10¢	25¢
$.01	$.05	$.10	$.25

$1
$1.00

$5
$5.00

$10
$10.00

$20
$20.00

1 Listen

A. Listen and point.

B. Listen and repeat.

2 Say

Listen. Repeat.

A: How much is this?
B: 75¢.
A: Thanks.
B: You're welcome.

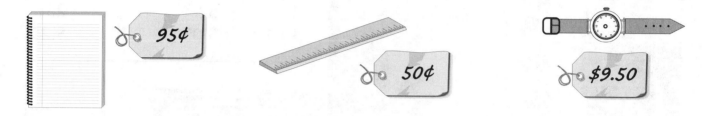

95¢

50¢

$9.50

Practice with a partner. Talk about these prices.

3 Read

pen—50¢

book—$3.95

tape—$1.19

glue—85¢

pad of paper—$1.25

box of paper clips—$1.09

Circle.

1.	$($1.25$)$	$1.50	$2.25
2.	$4.20	$2.10	$2.40
3.	$5.75	$5.25	$5.50
4.	$3.15	$3.40	$3.60

Match.

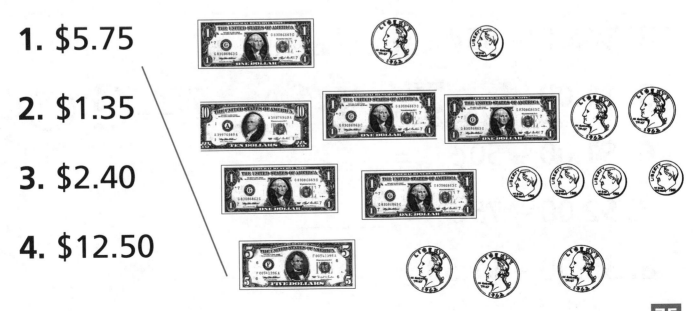

1. $5.75

2. $1.35

3. $2.40

4. $12.50

4 Write

A. How much?

1. <u>$6.75</u>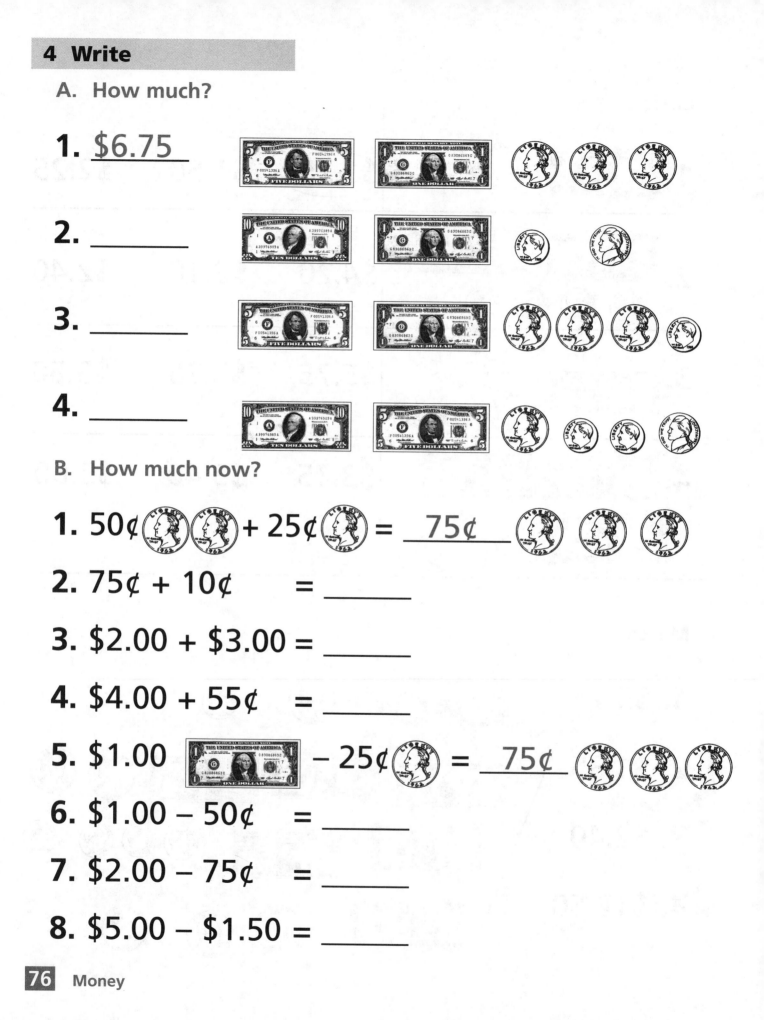

2. _____

3. _____

4. _____

B. How much now?

1. 50¢ + 25¢ = <u>75¢</u>

2. 75¢ + 10¢ = _____

3. $2.00 + $3.00 = _____

4. $4.00 + 55¢ = _____

5. $1.00 − 25¢ = <u>75¢</u>

6. $1.00 − 50¢ = _____

7. $2.00 − 75¢ = _____

8. $5.00 − $1.50 = _____

5 Listen and Speak

A: How much is it?
B: That's $3.00.
A: Here's $5.00.
B: $2.00 is your change.
A: Thank you.

Practice with a friend.

6 Read and Write

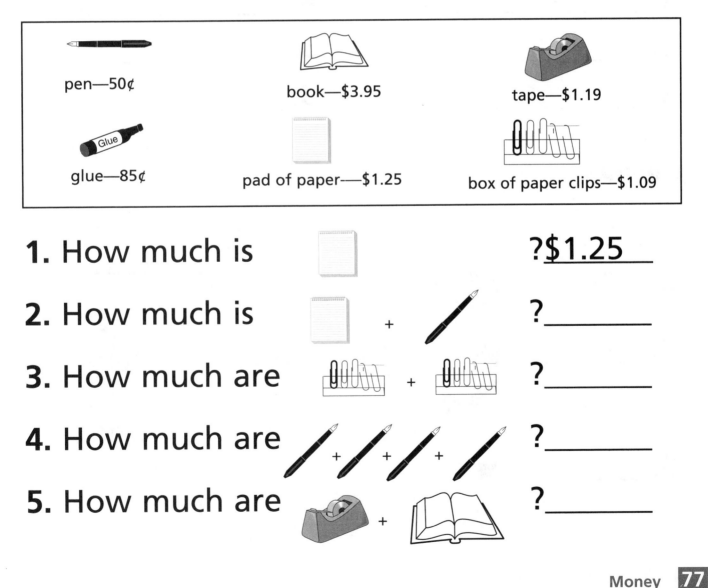

pen—50¢

book—$3.95

tape—$1.19

glue—85¢

pad of paper——$1.25

box of paper clips—$1.09

1. How much is ?**$1.25**

2. How much is + ?_____

3. How much are + ?_____

4. How much are + + + ?_____

5. How much are + ?_____

Numbers

1 Listen and Circle

1. $3.85   ($3.80) $3.15
2. $10.60 $7.50 $10.75
3. $9.25 $9.95 $5.95
4. $3.62 $3.16 $3.92

5. $11.40 $17.40 $11.70
6. $23.97 $32.90 $23.79
7. $18.10 $14.70 $18.90
8. $3.92 $6.50 $15.60

2 Listen and Write

1. $7.33
2. _____
3. _____

4. _____
5. _____
6. _____

3 Write

1. _____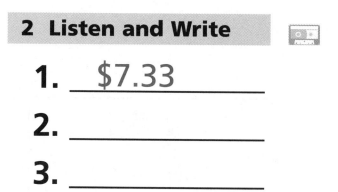

2. _____

3. _____

4. _____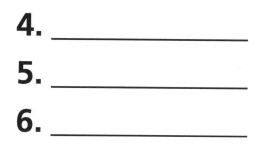

5. _____

Application

1 Pair Work

Ask a friend.

How much is it?
It's $2.75.

SALE! SALE!
Low Prices! Great Value!
Office and School Supplies

39¢

$2.25

$1.65

79¢

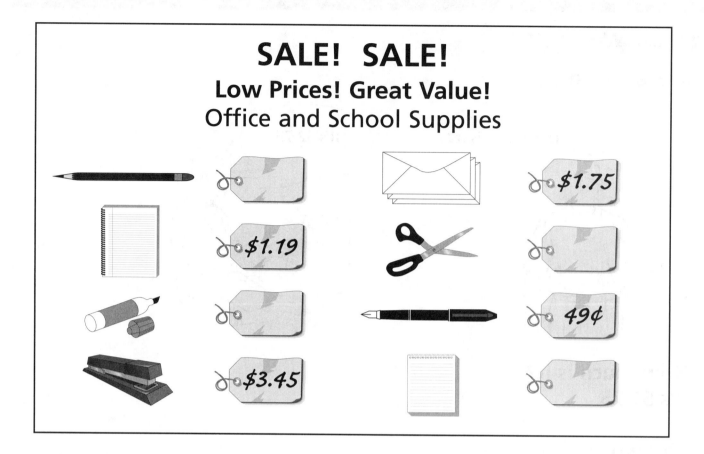

2 Culture Work

Unit 9
LET'S EAT

Openers

Look.

1 Listen

A. Listen and point.

B. Listen and repeat.

2 Say

Listen. Repeat.

A: I need <u>apples</u>.
B: They're in Aisle <u>1</u>.
A: Thanks.

A: I need <u>fish</u>.
B: It's in Aisle <u>3</u>.
A: Thanks.

Practice with a partner.

3 Read

SALE! SALE!
Low Prices! Great Value!

$2.49/ 1 bag

49¢/ 1 lb.

69¢/ 1 lb.

$3.75/ 1 lb.

75¢/ 1 head

$3.25/ 1 bag

$1.19/ 1 doz.

89¢/ 1 loaf

Circle.

1.		bread	(eggs) meat
2.		bananas	oranges apples
3.		fruit	lettuce fish
4.		rice	raisins meat
5.		tomatoes	chicken lettuce

Circle.

AISLE 1	**AISLE 2**	**AISLE 3**
oranges	bread	fish
tomatoes	rice	chicken
bananas		meat

1.   (AISLE 1)   AISLE 2   AISLE 3

2.   AISLE 1   AISLE 2   AISLE 3

3.   AISLE 1   AISLE 2   AISLE 3

4.   AISLE 1   AISLE 2   AISLE 3

5.   AISLE 1   AISLE 2   AISLE 3

4 Write

Write the prices.

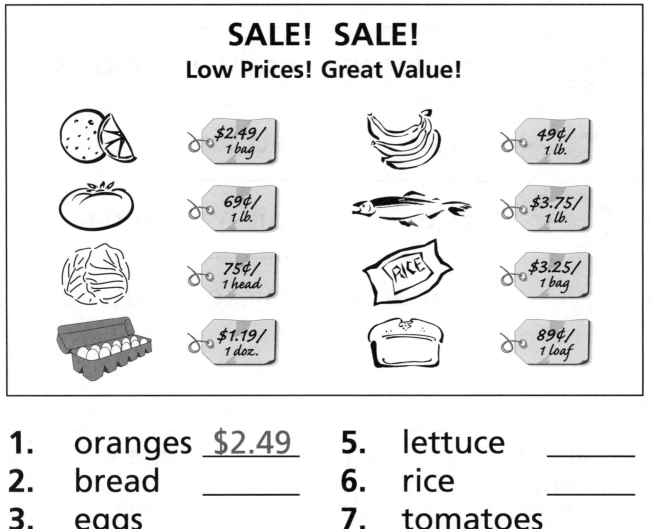

SALE! SALE!
Low Prices! Great Value!

$2.49/ 1 bag

69¢/ 1 lb.

75¢/ 1 head

$1.19/ 1 doz.

49¢/ 1 lb.

$3.75/ 1 lb.

$3.25/ 1 bag

89¢/ 1 loaf

1. oranges $2.49
2. bread _____
3. eggs _____
4. fish _____

5. lettuce _____
6. rice _____
7. tomatoes _____
8. bananas _____

5 Listen and Speak

A: How much is the fish?

B: $3.50 a pound.

A: How much are the eggs?

B: $1.19

Practice with a friend.

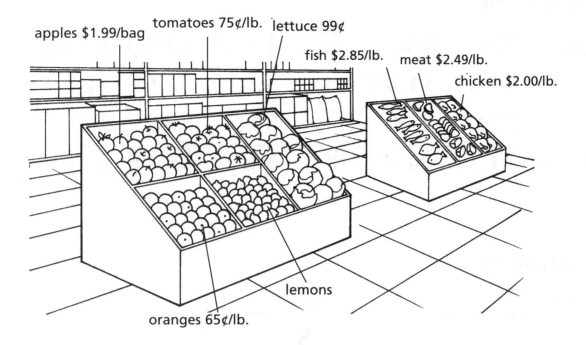

apples $1.99/bag
tomatoes 75¢/lb.
lettuce 99¢
fish $2.85/lb.
meat $2.49/lb.
chicken $2.00/lb.
lemons
oranges 65¢/lb.

1. How much is the fish? $2.85/lb.

2. How much are the oranges? _____

3. How much are the tomatoes? _____

4. How much is the chicken? _____

5. How much is the lettuce? _____

6. How much are the apples? _____

7. How much is the meat? _____

Numbers

1 Listen and Circle

1. 89¢ (79¢) 85¢
2. $1.15 $1.50 $1.40
3. 97¢ 57¢ 27¢
4. $3.49 $3.39 $4.39
5. $1.18 $2.80 $1.48
6. $2.29 $2.99 $2.19
7. 55¢ 65¢ 15¢
8. $4.09 $4.49 $2.89

2 Listen and Write

1. ____45¢____
2. _____
3. _____
4. _____
5. _____
6. _____

3 Write

How much is it?

1. bread _____
2. bananas _____
3. eggs _____
4. chicken _____
5. lettuce _____
6. rice _____
7. oranges _____
8. tomatoes _____

Ask. Write the prices.

Example: A: How much are the eggs?
         B: $1.09

Student A

Shop & Save Super Prices All Week!		
eggs $1.09	bread 65¢	 _____
  _____	apples $1.89	 _____
oranges $2.49	fish $3.25	 _____

Student B

2 Culture Work

88 Let's Eat

Picture Dictionary

Groceries

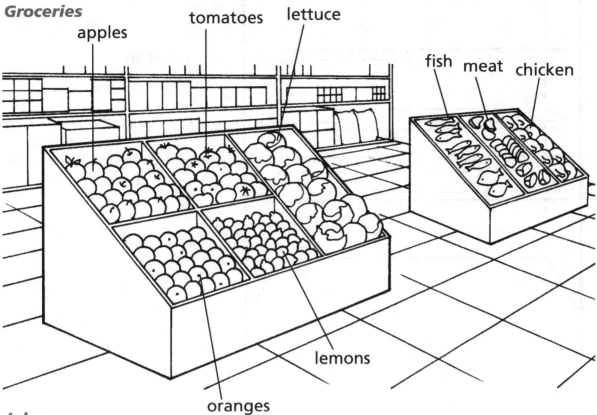

apples
tomatoes
lettuce
fish   meat   chicken
oranges
lemons

Jobs

an ambulance driver

an auto mechanic

a bus driver

a construction worker

a painter

a welder

Orientation and Direction

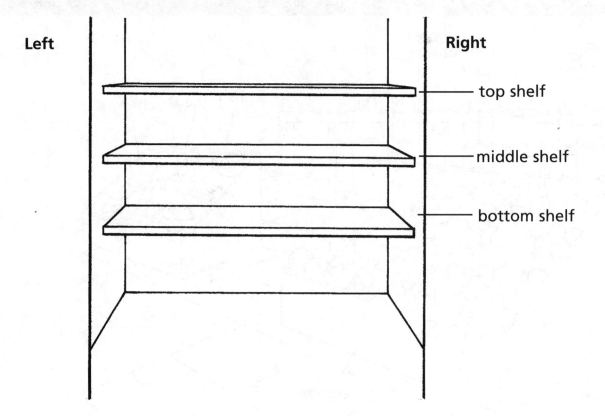

Left   **Right**

— top shelf

— middle shelf

— bottom shelf

Safety Signs

Exit

Danger

No Smoking

Radiation

Slow

Stop